If you have purchased this book without its cover, it may be a stolen book. This should be reported to the publisher.
This publication is written and is intended to provide reliable and competent information. Neither the publisher or the author is under any obligation to provide professional services in rendering financial, legal or any related book content advice or otherwise.
The law and practices vary from country to country and state to state. If legal or professional information is required, the purchaser or the reader should seek the information privately and best suited to their particular needs and circumstances.
The author and the publisher specifically disclaim any liability that may be incurred from the information and names used within this book.
The book contains a collection of case studies viewed from the researcher's perspective only. However, certain areas may have been enhanced for content purposes.
All rights reserved.
No part of this book, including the interior design, cover design, diagrams, or any intellectual property (IP) and icons may be reproduced or transmitted in any form by any means (electronic, photocopying, recording or otherwise) without the prior permission of the publisher.

ISBN: 978-0-6480836-1-0
Copyright© 2015 re-print 2017 Christine Thompson-Wells
All rights reserved.

Published by Planet Press International Ltd., under license from MSI Ltd, Australia

Company Registration No: 642923859
Australia

See our website: www.booksforreadingonline.com

Front & Back Covers and Copyright owned by MSI, Australia

| Content | Page |
|---|---|
| **Chapter One**<br>Why Should You Write A 'How To' Book? | 1 |
| **Chapter Two**<br>Getting Started | 12 |
| **Chapter Three**<br>The Future Of E-Books | 24 |
| **Chapter Four**<br>Now, Some Tips And Steps | 34 |
| **Chapter Five**<br>Finishing Off | 50 |
| **Chapter Six**<br>Don't Forget – Plan Your Book | 64 |

# Chapter One

## Why Should You Write A 'How To' Book?

I can remember my dear mother-in-law saying, *'I should write a book about life in Sydney.'* Sadly, she died without putting her ideas down on paper or ever writing her book!

My mother-in-law of course, was speaking about her life's experiences in Australia.

None of us need or 'have to' write a book but if we do, there is a sense of personal accomplishment, satisfaction and fulfilment of a task done!

Even in writing for pleasure, there is a feeling of accomplishment when the project is finished. On a more sombre note: if you write things down, your words may be read by future generations and that leaves you with the feeling: '….at least the effort you've put into your life has been worthwhile.'

Writing for pleasure is fine, but this current book you are going to write is about writing for a purpose. The purpose being: you are going to tell somebody else about you and what you can do; this could be the extra income you are looking for. This could also add value to your reader's life. With these thoughts, you are in the beginning stages of writing your first 'How To' book.

In giving you some ideas, are you aware, that everything that man or woman has ever made, created, or manufactured has started with somebody or a group of people coming up with a single thought?

Usually a thought is stimulated by a need within a human being somewhere, wanting or needing something to help them out of a situation or to make life a little bit easier or more comfortable?

This single thought sometimes leads to a collection of thoughts, and then an idea evolves or is born, this can develop into something being made, researched, or developed.

Everything made and used in every day life was just that, at one time: a thought that became an idea by somebody else. The chair you are sitting on was once somebody's idea. The shirt or jeans you are wearing were once, just an idea! An idea, however, can be worth a fortune! Just look at Bill Gates, he made his fortune through thinking 'How To' write software for computers. Henry Ford, through persistence of hard work and thinking, thought through the idea 'How To' developed the *'affordable motorcar!'*

I experienced a recession that took everything I had worked for, for over thirty years: my business, home, means of making my livelihood; I was left with little in material goods, however, I still had my mind and my thoughts.

My single thought being: 'I have to start again.' From a single thought came a collection of thoughts about the experiences I had gone through. The thoughts became the idea for writing my first 'How To' book on 'How To' become financially self-sustainable.

As a teacher, I knew there had to be answers to the way the 'World of Money' worked. Nobody could give me answers, not even bank managers in the 90's! We now know that even banks are liquidated, financially propped-up by other banks or governments, go bankrupt and cause recessions!

The more I see and think about the way money works in the world, the more I realise that there needs to be more people with knowledge about this subject. We all need to know 'How To' understand how money works. Not only do I now write *'How To'* books for adults on *'How To'* work with money, but I also write adventure stories that allow children to start and understand 'How To' work with money and the money concept.

When writing the money books, I didn't realise they would lead onto other areas of writing such as telling people how to sell or how to stay healthy – the scope for writing just becomes larger with the number of books I write.

So, it is with using my past experiences and knowledge, I write books for a living.

You will also need past experiences and knowledge to write your books. You will work your experiences and past knowledge into the 'Now' time. Your past knowledge and experiences will become the tools of your trade and combined-together, you will create and your first 'How To' book.

Remember, this book you are now reading, is giving you the framework in which to work, this book is a guide for the now and the future.

I know by reading this first chapter, you too, will start to think things through and start to create the framework for the topic you want to write about.

If at this point, you are a little stuck in starting to think the topics through, let's do it together.

Below are some topics that may give you ideas to get started.

If you love to cook:
- How to create 10 healthy budget meals for £10.00 or (AUD) $20.00.

If you enjoy gardening:
- How to plan and develop an autumn garden -

If you are a business consultant and are currently out of work:
- How to write a business plan.

Again, if you like baking:
- How to cook wholemeal bread and basic foods.

If you have been interested in wine making and have had some experiences in the industry:
- How to make affordable wine.

If your grandma left or gave you a recipe to make old fashioned jams and preserves:
- How to preserve fruit or make jams, the old-fashioned way.

If you have been a member of Toastmasters or such a group, have you thought about writing a 'How To' book on:
- How to compose and write your message and create the right image with public speaking.

If you have worked in an area where you have had to arrange corporate meetings:
- How to hold meetings.

If you are a teacher or an ex-teacher and want to bring in some extra money:
- How to write a letter or curriculum vitae.

If you have gone on a year's trip around the United States, Europe, Australia, or Asia -use the experience.
- A 'How To' Keep Safe, Does and Don'ts, Hints & Tips, camping sites and more.

If you have worked with craft projects, have you thought of writing on:

- How to make wicker baskets or stained-glass windows or stained-glass screens.

If you may have had some experience in making soap or candles:

- How many ways to make soap or candles?

What about traditional recipes such as scones and Victorian sponges that are different to the normal recipes:

- How to write a book on different recipes.

Writing a book on how to build dolls' houses could be for some people who enjoy this type of work.

- 20 easy steps to building a dolls' house.

For those of us who are not handy when the car breaks down.

- A 'How To' book for women drivers – keep it simple and I'm sure it would sell.

For those people who love to paint pictures:

- A 'How To' book on the first steps of painting for enjoyment

A different 'How To' book on body care:

- If you are studying nutrition what about a 'How To' eat well and know the 'food value' of the food, you eat?

If you have been making jewellery for some time:

- How to make and design jewellery.

If you have owned and operated a florist:

- How to become a florist.

If you have owned or run a day care centre for infants:

- How to operate a day care centre.

I make all sorts of Australian damper bread from fruit to cheese and people love it, so:

- A 'How To' book on something as simple as my damper bread would be a great starter if you are new to writing.

Every day, we are indeed acting out and doing 'How To' things; from doing the washing, making a meal, walking the dog and a hundred other things are all 'How To.' Each one of us has something that we do that is unique to us.

So now, take some time out, think of the things you could write a 'How To' book about and write them down below.

## Your Topics Of Interest

| My topic of interest to write about: |
|---|
| Topic One............................................................................ |
| Topic Two............................................................................ |
| Topic Three......................................................................... |
| Topic Four........................................................................... |
| Topic Five............................................................................ |
| Topic Six.............................................................................. |
| Topic Seven........................................................................ |
| Topic Eight.......................................................................... |
| Topic Nine........................................................................... |
| Topic Ten............................................................................ |

## Your Ten Tips

**Ten tips:**

1. Keep your idea simple
2. Keep your idea to yourself – telling other people allows you to lose your personal power. The more people you tell the weaker your idea becomes - I have learnt this by experience.
3. Keep working on your idea until it is crystal clear in your mind. Make notes and modify the notes daily.
4. Alcohol, nicotine and drugs will not allow you to think clearly when writing. When you are constructing sentences, the sentence needs to make sense and do something – they need to take the reader to another place; they need to take the reader on a journey. More about this in the next chapter.
5. You will need to be rested to write clearly. Looking after yourself physically and mentally makes it easier to write your book.
6. When you are in a muddle or feel 'muddle

headed' it is difficult to put sensible construction into sentences.

7. Keep the room quiet while you write. Noise, such as singing, or pop music can and does interfere with your mind. Your mind will have to work twice as hard to cope with the interference. With interference, you will also find, though you have been working hard, the task you have undertaken will be more difficult than it should be.

8. Give yourself regular breaks: work for twenty minutes, then drink some water or walk in the garden.

9. Once you have a substantial amount of work done, say every hour or two, give yourself a gift: pick a flower, make a hot chocolate or cup of tea or make that phone call you have been meaning to make.

10. Don't over do it. Work, but when your mind says 'enough is enough' make it enough.

# Chapter Two

## Getting Started

As a teacher of psychology and when working with people in high schools and higher education, I advise: '...work hard for at least twenty minutes and then have a *mind break* – look out of the window, sip some water and then start again.'

When you give your mind new information, your mind needs time to digest the information, channel and re-route the information into its different compartments.

All of this is unseen work and takes energy from your body. This energy originally starts with the food you eat. Simple: good whole food = clear thinking, easier workload, and more satisfaction from the task at hand.

With just the simple explanation above, you can see, that when starting to write a 'How To' book and to avoid unnecessary work, you need to be mentally ready for the project.

Trying to write, when you are not fully prepared mentally, will lead to frustration and giving up on the project. You don't want to do that and lose the momentum and opportunity of becoming who you

are really meant to be, also, you may lose the opportunity of creating a much needed, income!
So, with a clear head, you can now start your project.

Have some paper and a pen handy or work directly on to your computer – I do both.

Sometimes, when I'm alone and I'm eating my midday meal, I jot down notes while sitting at the dining room table; these notes come into my consciousness as my mind relaxes a little.

Also, I take little breaks from the computer and will do a house chore, like hanging out the washing. I know while doing this very ordinary housework task, my sub-conscious and conscious minds are working together. My mind is working to give me the answers I am looking for with my writing.

By working this way, slowly, slowly, I win the race!

If you have chosen your topic to write about, it's time to put some physical action into your project.

Write down the title of your book. This book I am writing is called, 'Why & How To Write a "How To" Book.'

Your book title may be: 'How To' Preserve Fruit - Victorian Recipes. This title may change over time, but for now, you have started.

If you are going to stay with the title you have chosen as in the above, there may be all sorts of combinations that could be used to preserve fruit: Honey and Fruit, Fruit and Liqueur, Fruit and Whiskey Combinations and many more!

Once the title is in place you can start to do your research. If you have your grandma's recipes that you want to use, research them; make them yourself and then try them out.

There is nothing better than to actually experience, 'by doing' the actual topic you are going to write about.

'By doing,' you are validating your information and adding credibility to your writing.

## Validate Your Writing

As a lifestyle psychologist, and having experienced the real effects of a recession, I can validate my writings and speak of the subject: Money Psychology. Other people find it difficult to verbally 'shoot you down,' when you have had the experience. Though people may not always agree with you, in some instances, you can become almost 'bullet proof.'

## Sentence Construction

Again, I am speaking from my teacher's mouth: Keep your sentences short and to one thought.

Remember, an idea is a collection of thoughts. To give you a starting point:

1. The cat sat on the mat. Easy, we know exactly what the cat has done: 'Sat on the mat.'

2. The black cat sat on the mat. Easy, we know now that it was a black cat.

3. The black and white cat sat on the mat. Easy, we now know that the cat was not only black but also white and was, at one point in time, (past tense) sat on the mat.

A simple sentence has been constructed that gives the reader a lot of information about a cat.

In all writing, we need to 'Keep it simple stupid.' It is the KISS factor in writing.

So many people cram many thoughts into one sentence. By doing this, the sentence becomes distorted and variations in the tone of the words may take place. A sentence needs to flow smoothly, be easy to read and understand.

Already, if your sentences aren't flowing and just by using your imagination, you can see the work your reader would have to go through to understand the topic you were writing about.

Your reader wants to enjoy your book and not feel, by the end of reading it, exhausted from the experience.

**Related Ideas**

When writing your chapters, if this is the way you have decided to write your book, keep your collection of related ideas to one chapter.

Remember:

- Keep each chapter to it's theme – for instance: you are speaking about the ageing of human skin:

- keep your words to the theme of ageing skin

- Always moving forward showing how ageing skin can be revived:

    - Eating correctly balanced meals, relaxation and exercise.

- The next chapter could include the types of creams to use and the following chapter

- How to massage and revive ageing skin.

Keep re-reading your words and keep in mind the essence of the story and moving ahead.

I try to write each chapter with the same or similar number of words in each chapter. This may be difficult to do at times; your chapter content or topic, to some degree, will dictate the number of words used in each chapter.

It is easy to check your word count. Under 'Tools' on the menu bar of your computer, click the menu bar, the comes down and says: Word Count, highlight the word number, click Word Count and keep your tally.

*Always remember,* you are taking your reader on a progressive journey from the beginning to the end of your book.

**The Journey Begins**

Once your topic is in place, you now formulate your plan. To formulate your plan, either on your computer or on separate pieces of paper, write your headings.

Mine for this book are:

- Formulating your plan
- Why should you write a book?
- Logical steps
- Getting started
- Clear thinking

- Meeting a need
- Writing my content
- Editing
- Pricing
- Intellectual property (IP)
- Copyright
- Marketing
- Distribution: internet, bookstores, website.

The above list will change as I work through and write the book. The list, however, is my framework and will help to keep me focused on my project. On starting my project, my framework is not always in its right order. As the book unfolds, I start to see the logical flow that is needed to keep the reader on their journey.

In the planning stages of writing your 'How To' book, you will need to ask yourself two simple questions:

1. What gives your 'How To' book an advantage over other 'How To' books in the marketplace?
2. What is the solution you are offering to your customer or client and how will it help them solve their problem?

*If you cannot solve a problem, then you are not writing a 'How To' book.*

By definition, and the nature of 'How To' books: a 'How To' book normally relates to the writer having the solution within the content of the book, for the customer or reader's dilemma or their problem.

When planning your book, you will need to keep this very valid point in mind.

With writing a 'How To' book on Making Ten Nutritional Meals for £10.00 or (AUD) $20.00 you would ask:

### Who Is In My Market Place?

Answer:

*Young families, students, people living on low, fixed, and non-flexible budgets or incomes, pensioners, and people that are out of work and so on.*

If you cannot answer: Who is in my market? You would need to re-evaluate your topic and possibly look for something else to write your book on.

Avoid the disappointment of this realisation early in the project; always, always *look to solve a problem* when planning to write your book. If there is not a problem, how do you identify the solution? Even more importantly, how do you write a 'How to Book?'

However, with the right research done at the beginning of your project, you will always find there is a person or situation that is looking for a solution to a problem.

If you are looking for a topic, look into the marketplace and see where there is a problem or a demand for a solution. Identifying the solution becomes your 'How To' book.

## Identifying Problems In The Market Place

You can identify problems in the Market Place by:

- ✓ Listening to the local news
- ✓ Reading the local newspapers
- ✓ Talking to people at local community centres
- ✓ Talking to people at local churches
- ✓ Talking to teachers and people who run children's groups

When you step 'outside of the box,' you have a better chance of identifying a need in the community.

There is always somebody, somewhere who would like somebody else to 'shine a light' on a problem they have.

## Timing

There is always a consumer or customer demand when there is a problem. The problem for writers' is identifying the problem at the right moment in time.

In the aggressive attacks of terrorism in 2001 on the Twin Towers in New York, people were looking for answers to 'Why?'

This is but one human area of severe distress, loss, and grief that, to this day, still needs attention.

There are many areas of human living and experience that can be written about.

Other areas of the 'need for knowledge' come about when people are diagnosed with severe illnesses and they want to identify with other people who have had a similar experience.

The 'need for knowledge' is insatiable and will not stop because human beings are always looking for answers or solutions to problems.

The ever active 'human spirit' is within us all, it's always demanding; it wants to know more and once the answer is found, another question will show itself!

You may be fortunate enough to be given some time out by the human spirit, but sooner or later there will be another demand made on you.

Human beings, working with the human spirit, like to know there is a way forward. People like to know there are possible answers to their experiences.

Because of the nature of human beings, they like to know and can take some comfort when they can identify, read about or hear the story of another person experiencing a similar situation.

## Niches In The Market Place
## Demand?

Like 'Timing,' you also need to look at 'Niches In The Market Place.'

Is your work, before it's written, going to meet the 'Needs' of your marketplace? Is another question that you need to ask yourself?

Also ask yourself, before you put any more effort into your project: 'am I aiming at a Niche market or is there a popular demand for what I am writing about?'

Look for your answers. Do some research on the internet and tick or cross the boxes below.

## Identify Your Topic

| Yes  | Popular | Cannot |
|------|---------|--------|
| Need | Demand  | Decide |
|      |         |        |

**Cannot Decide:** If you are in the box of cannot decide: look for another topic.

**Popular Demand:** If it is a popular demand market, the market may also be flooded with other people trying to sell their books on the same topic you want to write about. If your work takes a different slant, you may, however, just strike it lucky in this marketplace.

**Yes, Need:** If you identify there is a '*Need*,' then write as quickly as you can and get your book out there and into the marketplace.

# Chapter Three

## The Future Of E-Books

Because I am now in the world of publishing, it pays me to keep my 'finger on the pulse' of the publishing world.

So, what is an e-book? An e-book is a downloadable book through the internet; it is an electronic book. For instance, if you write a book and publish it as an e-book, you would not necessarily go through the traditional channels of publishing, printing and then physical distribution of your book and into bookshops.

You can write your own e-book and publish on-line as I'm doing with this book.

Technology is rapidly expanding; we now have e-readers and other technology that is making the publishing world change.

Traditional paper book publishing has had 'market dominance' for many years but with new technology e-books are becoming popular.

During 2009, there were about two million e-books sold annually. In 2012, for the first time ever, e-books outstripped the sales of paper back books and the market is continually growing.

This changing publishing world is 'free market' competition and is a good opportunity for you to get your books into the marketplace.

To assist you with your book sales, the manufacturers of software like the Bill Gates of this world, are now manufacturing e-book readers and other effective devices which will allow more books to be sold.

So you can see with the above information, the possibility of your potential market place, more importantly: the number of books you can possibly write and sell to other people is of worldwide proportions.

If you have dreamed of becoming a writer but the road has been too difficult please just keep reading on. Sometimes, we fall down with our dreams because we cannot see a way forward; I could have given up many times!

So you now know that if you are to write a 'How To' book there are certain criteria for you to meet to make it a saleable book.

**Lifestyle**

As I have previously outlined, a 'How To' book is written to help somebody, somewhere solve a problem or find a solution to make changes in their life! Yes, changing lifestyles, changing thinking patterns, changing habits, and in some instances, empowering people to become who they are meant to be.

If you like, you are *'cracking the life-long nut'* of your reader. The nut may have encapsulated them hampering their personal growth. You may be helping them to find their freedom in thinking and possibly the actions and habits they have adopted over their lifetime and this is all done through the power of the written word.

The human race has been aware of the power of the written word since before the time of Socrates four hundred years before the birth of Christ and the power of the written word will continue while we, as human beings, have the power to think!

The power of thinking is the power that drives me on. My money psychology books are written about:

- ✓ changing lifestyle for my reader
- ✓ taking control
- ✓ creating a better life for my reader and their family
- ✓ self-satisfaction and
- ✓ personal growth.

My books are also about, the reader becoming aware that they have the power within them to:

- ✓ Move from one negative situation and into
- ✓ A positive 'now' and a fulfilling future.

So, is your 'How To' book about changing lifestyles, about showing somebody else, possibly on the other side of world about doing something that will enhance their life for the better?

By giving somebody a little extra knowledge for example: about finding a diet that really works for them? Or have you discovered a skin preparation which is unique and affordable? This skin preparation may change somebody's lifestyle for now and the future?

- Can you justify the words you are writing about?
- Do you have some proof about the information you are writing about?
- Do you have testimonials you can use to validate your information?

If you were to write a book on 'How To' *Relax Through Times Of Great Personal Trauma And Stress*; this book could make the difference between life or death for somebody, somewhere!

Ask yourself: 'Can I validate the words I write about?'

By your knowledge being imparted to another person, you have indeed contributed to somebody's lifestyle and possible well-being.

So, there are two questions you need to ask yourself now:

1. How will my 'How To' book make somebody else's life better?
2. How will I save them time and money through them buying my book?

## Must Have

As you plan the book, ask yourself '...am I writing a **'Must Have'** book or are you just hoping it will work?'

To plan a **'Must Have'** book you will need to think 'outside of the box' and think of something as revolutionary and as different as the Dr Atkins Low Carb Diet books. These books are 'How To' and became 'Must Haves'. Other ideas do come to mind: *Recipes for 2070 – 'Food Ideas For The Future.'* But the question has to be asked: would Food Ideas For The Future become a 'Must Have' book? It would be a 'How To' book but without the right marketing and timing in place; it could fall short of becoming a 'Must Have' book.

## Quirky books

Planning a quirky book is not so difficult and is still a tangible product that can be written by you and sold as an e-book. Some quirky books do become best sellers but again, need the right marketing and timing in place.

Books which come to mind under the *Heading of Quirky Books are:*

- Animal Farm
- St Lucy's Home For Girls Raised By Wolves
- Lord Of The Flies
- The Cat's Table
- The Pet Rock Series and more

Quirky books are fun to right especially if they hold within their pages: *'the answer to a problem.'*

## Staying In Control

In writing books or e-books you stay in control of your own book and the marketing of the book. When writing for a publisher, you can feel that you have little to no control of your work.

If you are working on a budget and know that you have the time and knowledge to put into your book, start writing now.

Don't become despondent, if you read your first chapter and it sounds like some sort of archaic language; it will get better as you read and re-read re-type and re-type your work!

Yes, writing a book is not for the *'faint hearted!'* It means writing, re-writing and re-writing again and again.

Some of our books have as many as eleven edit runs through them, and still, with the last edit, a line or word shouts at you from the pages you are looking at!

My editor, John, has said, 'expect as many as eight typos or missed edits in every piece of writing that goes out.' Of course, we try to find everything that is not right, but I am 'only human' and so are you.

So, don't be too hard on yourself in the beginning.

With staying in control of your work, it puts more responsibility on you to perform and produce your book.

In the traditional hard copy, paper book market, when writers were paid on a commission base by a publishing house, authors were paid a fee up front and then wrote their book. The royalties paid would be between 10 and 12% of the *net* revenue of the publisher.

Some writers were lucky if they ever saw any money from the hard work and long hours of toil they put into their work. Some, like JK Rowling have made a fortune but her case is indeed rare.

In staying in control of your work and publishing yourself, after paying your immediate expenses such as an editor if he or she has helped you, you are entitled to all of the payments for your books. That proposition is far more acceptable than receiving 10 or 12% of any *net profit* made by a publisher. A publisher does, however, *have the essential route-to-market!*

## Timing, Again

There is a time for a topic to be written and read by the marketplace and a time when you should not waste your valuable time on writing something that has been done to death previously.

This is a judgement call on your part.

Harry Potter has been written, read, filmed and it is possibly at saturation point. This saturation point, indeed, does cause a market vacuum. However, the vacuum will only be filled again, when the timing is right, and nobody knows when that time is exactly right! Even Nigel Newton, Chief Executive of Bloomsbury Publishing, (publishers' of the Harry Potter series) is unable to say when the next 'big book' frenzy will take place!

Looking for the 'next big idea' will put you into a positive place for writing your book. Search for the 'Market Demand' on Google websites and source your information from the internet. The internet is a powerful tool that we can all use to our advantage.

So, the way ahead for the self-published book writer looks rewarding. If, as a writer, you manage to hit a 'Must Have' 'How To' book at the right time in the marketplace, you will create many sales over a period of set time. Books, e-books and paper backs have their time and the time comes to an end, however, getting it right can make somebody very wealthy.

The secret here is have your ideas ready to produce your next book before the sales of the first one start, fade and stop.

## A few points to remember:

1) For a book to be successful it must fill a 'Need' of the customer or consumer.
2) If you can write a 'Must Have' 'How To' book, the sky is your limit.
3) Quirky books such as the *'Pet Rock'* series can become best sellers' but they are not 'How To' books but can become 'Must Haves.'
4) By staying in control of your work, you can have far greater monetary returns from your work but all of the responsibility for the 'success' or 'no success of the book lies with you.
5) The timing of your book is essential if it is to become successful. Nobody, not even

publishers who are in the publishing industry *can tell if they are publishing a best seller or a flop* – it appears all to be a matter of chance and luck.

# Chapter Four

## Now, Some Tips And Steps

I first determine my title page. As I write, the book title may change through the evolution and growth of the book. By the time the book reaches the marketplace, the name may have changed many times.

Secondly, I write a list of Chapters starting with Chapter One and go through to ten or twelve, just like below:

**Chapter One**
**Why Should You Write A 'How To' Book?**

**Chapter Two**
**Getting Started**

**Chapter Three**
and so on.

By doing this, I give myself even further direction. I normally have about ten chapters listed, sometimes the book is shorter and sometimes longer; I just add or delete chapter headings as I go.

I always write the chapter heading to begin with, in this instance: Why Should You Write A 'How To'

Book? Seeing each heading in its place, gives me the inspiration to keep writing.

As I write the chapter content, I refer back to my chapter heading, by doing this, it allows me to keep moving on with the essence of the chapter. This method of working leads me on and gives me the groundwork for the next chapter.

I keep the words moving forward, always taking my reader on their journey of discovery.

By moving forward and not allowing myself to get 'bogged down,' it allows me to have a sense of achievement and accomplishment with my writing.

By writing the Chapter Heading it gives me the scope in which to work. Every person has a different style of working; this is a style that works for me.

Every book that I write has its own personality. *Making Cash Flow* is so completely different to *39 Steps & 39 Days to Debt Recovery* or *Discover Your Selling Power* and *Adam's Mind – Eve's Psyche.* Each book has its own character and frame of reference.

The children's books I write also, start at the beginning like the adult books but then, as I write, the book starts to develop a personality of it's own and are, for me, very refreshing to create.

As you write, you will find out more about yourself and your personality – you will indeed grow from within. You will also get cross when you think you have written something that is complete nonsense, but even nonsense writing has its purpose. So, try not to be too demanding of yourself in the first place.

## Intellectual property (IP)

I have mentioned ICE earlier in the book. ICE is the Intellectual Content Expo that is held annually in Toronto, Canada. I found the experience of going to ICE very stimulating and extremely informative.

One point to mention here is the value of Intellectual Property or (IP). Many people, indeed, possibly thousands of people over the centuries, have lost their IP to rogues, scoundrels' or to people who haven't got the intelligence to write something for themselves.

These rogues, scoundrels and fraudsters lack in personal integrity and personal values – the only way forward for them, is to steal from a writer!

Since writing, I have experienced many people wanting to have a part of the content or the IP. In some instances, people can 'Spin' a good story and are so completely convincing that we, as writers, can be lured into the competition when we feel desperate about getting our work published.

I too, speak from experience. I have been hoodwinked, and told a very good tale, even to the point where the 'story teller,' wanted £12,000 up front and the complete ownership of all of my current written work and any work I should write in the future. This was a harsh experience and cost me a lot of time and money.

My warning here is for you.

I now only write for myself and stay in control of the work I do. I work with three different approaches:

1. I write the first draft
2. Re-read the first draft
3. Print it out in hard copy

This hard copy becomes the Master copy and is backed up on the computer in at least three different places, maybe five!

Copy at least one copy onto a CD or USB and store it in a fire-resistant cabinet.

**Create A New Folder And Title It: 3 Part Printer Copy.**

Then divide the original copy, still on the computer, into three different sections:

**First Section:**

You need to create a File, title it: File 1 *Front and Back Cover*. Design your front and back covers.

You can use Word A5 or A4 paper size but make sure the cover copy is the same size as your book, either A5 or A4.

Sample A5 Book Cover

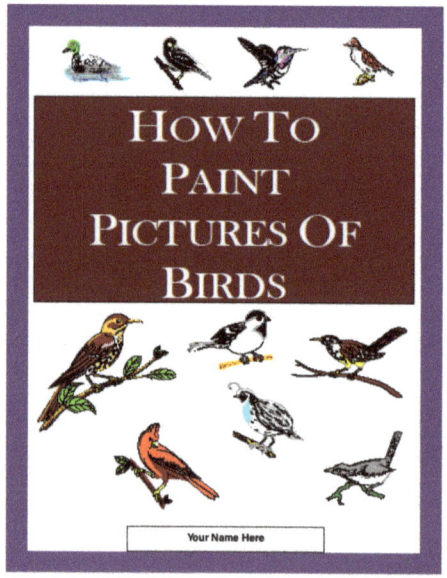

On the internet, there is a great variety of clip art or individual photographs available - some is free, some, needs to be bought.

*Your book cover is the <u>emotional</u> connection to your readers' desire to buy your book!*

Book covers need to look clean, appealing and be something that will enhance your reader's life.

a. **Have a Design in Mind for the Front and Back Covers,** save and store in File 1. By having a frontpage design in mind for your book, it keeps you focused, and you will feel the excitement and challenge for your project. Title the File: Front and Back Book Covers, store in the **3 Part Printer Copy Folder – How To Paint Pictures Of Birds 2012)**. Always date your folder.

Designing your book cover can be done when you are working through your book or at the end of your writing, or when you need to do a bit of 'day dreaming' while your mind is working out the next move to make or word to write!

See the above sample book cover.

**Second Section:**

b. **Write the Foreword and Chapter Title Content Pages (Save** and store in File 2, title the file: Foreword & Title Content Page – store in the **3 Part Printer Copy Folder)**

Other 'How To' books by
Christine Thompson-Wells:
**Discover Your Selling Power
Selling Made Easy
Making Cash Flow
39 Steps & 39 Days To Debt Recovery
Money Management For Students
How To Find Your Mind Of Gold
Adam's Mind – Eve's Psyche
The Psychology Of Money
How To Write Your Own How To Book
And
Many 'How To' Children's Books**

Christine only believes in writing books that have a purpose – her books are intended to assist people to become self-sustainable.

The purpose of her journey, as a writer, is to enrich the world of her readers.

---

If you have purchased this book without its cover, it may be a stolen book.
This should be reported to the publisher.
This publication is written and is intended to provide competent information for adults. Neither the publisher nor the author is under any obligation to provide professional services in rendering any further information or otherwise.
The author and the publisher specifically disclaim any liability that may be incurred from the information within this book.
All rights reserved. No part of this book, including the interior design, cover design may be reproduced or transmitted in any form by any means (electronic, photocopying, recording or
otherwise) without the prior permission of the publisher. ISBN : 978-0-9873523-2-3
Copyright © 2012 including all illustrations belong to Christine Thompson-Wells
Masterclips (1999) IMSI http://www.imsiuk.co.uk (UK)
All rights reserved. Published under licence from Money School International Ltd (Australia) through Planet Press,
PO Box 745, Burpengarry, Queensland 4505, Australia
Company Registration No: 121 353 106 (Australia) First Edition 2012
Edited and laid out by John Firth.
Printed and bound by MBE Maroochydore,
Queensland, Australia

Sales: www.booksforreadingonline.com

*Dedicated To Doris Wells*
*Sydney, Australia*

### From The Author

*Why should you write a book?*

*Many people sadly die and with them dies a lifetime of history and experience.*

*Writing books is not an easy process and it takes many hours of 'crafting your story,' which eventually allows you to move on with writing your words down and eventually, you have, a finished book.*

*If you have a feeling or you keep receiving the message: 'write this down!' you should listen to the words or feelings your are experiencing.*

*Writing is an investment in your lifetime. It's something which you or your children, grandchildren can look at in the future, writing ultimately, is the picture you paint of the life you have lived.*

*I know from being a writer, there is always somebody, somewhere wanting the information I have. This knowledge keeps me writing and thinking and asking: what do I need to write about now?*

*Yes, writing can be heavy going and exhausting but at the end of the writing there comes unimaginable rewards in self-satisfaction and fulfilment.*

*I wish you all the best with writing and hope you achieve your goals; this book has been written with that intention in mind.*

*Thank you.*

*Christine*

| **Chapter One**<br>Why Should You Write A Book? | **Page**<br>2 |
|---|---|
| **Chapter Two**<br>Getting Started | 14 |
| **Chapter Three**<br>The Future Of E-Books | 26 |
| **Chapter Four**<br>Now, Some Tips And Steps | 36 |
| **Chapter Five**<br>Finishing Off | 52 |
| **Chapter Six**<br>Don't Forger – Plan Your Book | 66 |

The second file contains all of the above.

## Third Section:

***c.*** **Book Content** – This is the whole story you have been working on (Save and store in File 3, title the file: *Content* – store in the *3 Part Printer Copy folder)*

**Why Should You Write A Book?**

I can remember my dear mother-in-law saying, 'I should write a book about life in Sydney.' Sadly, she died without putting her ideas down on paper or ever writing her book!

My mother-in-law of course, was speaking about her life's experiences in Australia.

None of us need or 'have to' write a book but if we do, there is a sense of personal accomplishment, satisfaction and fulfilment of a task done!

Even in writing for pleasure, there is a feeling of accomplishment when the project is finished. On a more sombre note: if you write things down, your words may be read by future generations and that leaves you with the feeling: '....at least the effort you've put into your life has been worthwhile.'

Writing for pleasure is fine, but this current book you are going to write is about writing for a purpose. The purpose being: you are going to tell somebody else about you and what you can do; this could be the extra income you are looking for. This could also add value and enrichment to your reader's life.

A sample content of the first page of the book.

By keeping your files separate as described in the above, they are ready to give to a printer for printing.

Keep your Master Separate and Save in a Separate File and Folder. Title your Folder: (I will title the folder: *How To Paint Pictures Of Birds;* keep this as a Separate File in its own separate Folder - always date your work as you add new information.

If you are tempted to go down the route where you are handing over your IP to another person, for instance a publisher or investor, here are some tips:

- ✓ Read everything on the paperwork given to you.
- ✓ Listen to the words you are hearing.
- ✓ Stay in control and always put the symbol © on your work.

Always be aware of protecting your IP, there are many people looking for IP or content. Content is the substance that makes the money for filmmakers, singers, television programmes, plays' performed on the stage and is used constantly in all forms of media.

IP is also in patenting of inventions, research and other forms of information such as software development, recipe books, even in the Bird book example above; IP is in everything which is developed through creativity.

So, content comes in many forms.

All media is made up of *Content* and is the information used in entertainment. Films, television, theatre, these are all content driven.

In many areas of the media, the content can be very shallow and leaves the viewer or the listener thinking or asking: 'What was that all about?' They may also think, 'I've paid good money, wasted my valuable time to listen to, look at or read rubbish – what a waste?'

Good content is what makes IP valuable. As a writer, you will need to always be aware of this.

Creative book content can be used to make films, videos, TV serials, electronic games, downloads for computers and other devices.

**Proceeding – Going To The Next Step**

**A Hypothetical Story:**

You have a vague idea of how long your book is going to be and have decided what form its going to take. You have decided to use your grandma's recipes. This is now the start and development of the 'How To' book.

You are now thinking, '….in the first part or half of the book, I could write about the story of Grandma's recipes.' You continue to think: ' …the story could include how she used these recipes before and during the Second World War.'

You are now giving your reader the background by creating the story; this takes care of the first pages of the book. You are still deciding and ask yourself: '...do I put all of the recipes into this first book or keep some of them for another book?'

Your Grandma was a very methodical woman and kept her recipes safe and protected over her lifetime. At the time of her death, she had accumulated about a hundred or more.

I would suggest, don't put all of the recipes into your book at one go. If your book is successful, the remaining recipes could be used in later books. By doing this and informing your reader: *'that more recipes will be coming in later books,'* you will create a following and your readers, if they like the book, will be anxious to buy the next copy that you publish.

This is a great feeling; you can see the way forward and know that you are creating something that could be of value to you or to you and your family.

You continue to work and write and stay vigilant and focused on your project.

As I have said, 'don't talk about your project; keep your energy within you.' From experience I know I need to amass vast amounts of personal energy and inspiration to keep moving my project forward. To keep moving forward, I need:

- ✓ Dedication
- ✓ Momentum
- ✓ Anticipation
- ✓ Excitement and the
- ✓ Confidence to finish the book.

As you are getting closer, and to the end of your work, your mind may wonder, and you may start to think: *'how much can I sell my work for?'*

The excitement builds, and it's difficult, at this point, to stay focused on the project. This is your mind starting to get a little out of control. This is also the 'Child' part of your personality showing itself.

Yes, it's great to get excited, but you still need to finish the project!

You can think about pricing when you are almost finished, but until it's finished you will need to contain your excitement.

On the day you complete the writing, by all means, give yourself a reward: cook a nice meal, enjoy a glass of wine, go to the cinema; do something that rewards you for the effort you have dedicated to your project.

We all need to recognise a great feat when it is accomplished.

# Chapter Five

## Finishing off

You have finished writing your project. You are constantly editing and going over the work looking for mistakes or typos. You think the work is fine, but you are not certain about some parts and would like a second opinion.

From past-experience, it is difficult to find our own mistakes. A mistake to one of your reader's could shout out loudly from the pages of your book.

I constantly look for my mistakes and know they are within the pages, but my eyes continually skim over them. Mistakes may come in the tone of the sentence, the way I use colloquialisms, (colloquialisms are those words or phrases that are used in the culture of our individual and everyday language).

If you are a little hesitant to go to the next stage, the selling stage, have somebody else look over your work.

There are professional editors and proof-readers that will do the job for a fee.

## Pricing Your Work

If you are going to market and sell your own book as a self-publisher, you will need to think about pricing. If you have undergone expenses, you will need to consider:

1. How long the work has taken to prepare?

2. If using other people, what you have invested in editing fees, illustrations, photography, or other fees incurred?

You will also need to know how many books you need to sell to get your invested money back.

When a person writes a book, they may do it for one of two good reasons:

1. They want to write the book to let other people know their experiences and they are not necessarily worried about making money, or
2. They are writing to bring in an income and writing is a valid way of creating your livelihood.

A word of caution, if you want to retain your customers and want them to buy again, you need to keep your pricing reasonable.

You will need to research and look at the comparisons of your products to others that are similar in the marketplace.

It isn't any good putting a price on the product that is too high for the actual value of the product.

I want to ask you a question: 'Would you rather sell 500 books at £5.00 or 1,000 at £3.50?

Of course, higher volume and lower profit will always win over in the number of books or products sold and the profit you make. So, you will need to think about this and bear this in mind.

*Please take note: you have little to no control over the pricing of your work if you are going through a publishing company.*

## Staying In Control

## Self Publishing – Your Website

If you are going to the marketplace and want to sell your own book and later books, one of the less expensive ways to do it is through your own website. If you haven't got a website, there are affordable templates and 'do-it-yourself' websites available to buy.

If you are however, a little like me, though I use a computer, I am not technically minded. I do, however, continue to try and work with new software as it becomes available, but I still have a website designer develop the website.

To keep the costs down, I do all of the writing and roughly design the website, the web designer and I then work together to achieve what I can see in my mind.

If you want to sell your book from your website, you will need to put a secure payment system into place. PayPal offer this facility, go to: https://www.paypal.com

Other payment sites are available.

However, before getting to the payment stage and if your are going to want to get your book into the bigger market on the high street you will need to know about ISBN numbers and legal deposits.

## ISBN Numbers

If you want to sell your books in hard paper copy to bookshops you will need have an ISBN number allocated to each book that you write and later publish. ISBN numbers are the identifiable numbers relating to your book. A bar code is produced from the number sequencing relating to your ISBN number.

ISBN numbers are bought from an ISBN Agency, in the United Kingdom you can go to:

www.isbn.agency@neilsen.com and – Thorpe Bowker: www.thorpe.com.au/isbn in Australia.
You will need to buy the ISBN number first, before a barcode can be allocated to the written book.

ISBN numbers are not cheap, they cost between £8.00 and £10.00 each or £80.00 plus VAT for a batch of ten or (AUD $10.00 each or $80.00 plus GST for a batch of ten).

*Not all products require an ISBN number, you will need to access the information that you need from one of the above websites.*

## Barcodes

Once you have bought your batch of ISBN numbers, a set of numbers will need to be associated with a barcode.

Barcodes can be bought at many locations. I normally buy mine from Axicon at www.axicon.com. In the United Kingdom and in Australia, the printer of the books will access the barcode and possibly charge you for the service

A single barcode, including VAT, will cost a little under £15.00 (AUD about $30.00)

## Printing The Hard Copy Book

When your book is completed: read, edited for the eight or eleventh time, you may revise your book cover or feel happy enough with the first attempt you made! You have bought your ISBN numbers and your barcode; you can now contact the printer to print your book.

I ask Axicon to send to my printer the barcode and to cc: me into the sent email. The reason I do this: it is easy to corrupt a barcode and I can do this very easily!

If you do not know where to put the barcode, just call into any bookshop or supermarket and look at the back of any book. You will see where most publishers place this identification mark or symbol.

## Legal Deposits

Every book written, published, and sold should be registered through the Agency for Legal Deposit Libraries (ALDL) in the United Kingdom.

You can also contact: legaldeposit.org.uk or if you are living in Australia, go to the National Library of Australia at www.nla.gov.au.

In the United Kingdom, Six books are required to meet the legal requirements of legal deposit. All, six books are sent to: The National Library of Scotland Building, Causewayside, Edinburgh. As this is a new location for the Agency, you will need to check the address before sending your books.

Your books will be placed in the Legal Deposit Office, the British Library, the Bodleian Library, Oxford, the University Library, Cambridge, the National Library of Scotland, the Library of Trinity College, Dublin and the National Library of Wales, Aberystwyth.

**You are reminded: that one copy of every publication is legally mandated to be deposited free of charge at the British Library Deposit Office within One Month of Publication.**

**In overseas locations, please seek the requirements or your country**

Do please check all of the above information before depositing your books. All of the above information does change, and statutory changes are not the responsibility of the author or publisher, but you will need to keep up to date with this information.

### Printing Your Book

You will need to shop around for pricing. Print pricing can vary dramatically from one area to another.

Over the years, I have tried many printers. I must say, they have all done a good job to date. However, the prices printer's charge to print the book have made the difference. In some instances, when we have had books printed in a hurry, the printing has cost the same price as the suggested recommended retail price (RRP) of the book. This is not a financially 'cost effective' way to go.

In shopping around, before committing yourself to a printer, thinking smartly, this could save you a lot of money.

## Marketing

This is where the greatest 'stumbling block' can come about. Through years of searching and trying to uncover *'How To Get Our Books Into The Market Place'* we have found some of the pathways.

Once you have your ISBN number and barcode in place you can move to marketing.

Through years of attending international book fairs and going to different shows, we have found a route into the bookshops in the high street. Of course, these suggestions and our experiences are not a guarantee that your books will be bought by book shops, but at least it is a starting point.

When attending the last International London Book Fair, I had an appointment with a Nielsen Book Data representative. From speaking to the woman, I found out about the Nielsen Enhanced Book Listing Service. This service is a little under £200.00 a year (AUD $400) and would be well worth it if you were thinking of publishing more than one book.

The service offers you a dedicated editor that is able to help you directly if you have problems. The service also offers other benefits, go to: www.nielsenbookdata.co.uk then follow the links to Publishers and Distributors.

With the Nielsen Enhanced Book Service your name and book title goes onto different registers that High Street booksellers have access to.

Marketing of the product and book – **getting it to market** – is the most difficult part of the process that we have experienced.

If you have undergone difficulties in this area, the above information might just be the missing link!

## Working With A Publisher

I have mentioned previously about writing for or working with a publisher. There are some advantages to this way of going into the marketplace.

The established publisher has links, and knowledge of the publishing industry – they know many people and contacts that could possibly help with selling your book.

Like everything that goes through a third party, agent or representative, there is always a cost involved. The agent, publisher or third party is not going to miss out on making some money, but the bottom line could be, you may be the person missing out on making money if your book is successful!

Publishers have avenues into the marketplace that beginning writers do not have or know about. The lack of this knowledge and experience can lead to great expense, frustration and giving up on the idea of writing your book. This is why, sometimes, going with a publisher seems like an easier route forward.

When a publisher takes on a piece of writing for publication, there are clauses in the contract that state words to the effect: 'first option of your future work, etc, etc.'

This means, that if your work is successful with this publisher, they have legally an obligation from you, to have the first option to all of your future writing. You are legally tied and cannot move away from that publisher. If you are not successful, you are not going to care or you will perhaps wonder, '...if, my work had been with another publisher, would it have been a success?'

Also remember, the royalty payment, in most instances is 10% to 12% of the *net profit* of the publisher. This means, that after the publisher takes all of his or her expenses from the wholesale (not the retail price) of your book, you will be paid from the monies left over.

If the publisher has published your book and the book is losing money, your net royalties will be zero because the publisher has not made a profit!

As previously discussed, some authors do make great amounts of money, but they are rare indeed.

## Publishing With A Publisher

Many new writers want to write and 'don't know what to do next!' They have a vast collection of words written on the paper and sitting in front of them; they look at their work and effort and become bewildered by the processes they have gone through to get so far!

Some publishing houses offer their services to edit, print, publish and market your book. The cost of going to this type of publisher ranges from £400.00 to over £11,000.00 or (AUD $800 to $22,000).
However, there are still no guarantees, with such an expense, that your book will be a success.

## Publishing The e-Book From Your Own Website

This is by far the most exciting aspect of the publishing process to date.

As a writer, with e-book publication we stay in control of our work, our marketing, our income and distribution.

It's simple, we write the book once, load it up into an e-book and put it out through our website and into the marketplace.

Or is it simple?

**Our Tips:**

1. Write your book and keep in a Word document.

2. Edit your book. If you feel you miss typos or mistakes, get somebody else to go through your work.

3. We have used Nvu to compile our Word files into HTML files ready to be made into e-books.

   Nvu is free, off the internet, downloadable software and we found it excellent to use.

   (Please continually check for new software becoming available on the internet) Nvu, may not be for you!

   Please note: Where we found it difficult, when we were learning about e-books and because we have large numbers of illustrations drawn by our artist illustrator, was with inserting the illustrations into our Word document that was in HTML format.

It is easy to create HTML files. Instead of saving your files as you normally would in Word, go to the File menu on the left of your computer screen, click the menu down and go to Save as Web File; click this and you will see your document format change. This is now a Web and HTML File and suitable to uploading into an e-book

4. E-book software is used to transfer your book into an e-book that you can sell from a website on the internet.

We have also used E-Book Gold and found it to be excellent.

E-Book Gold is not free and costs a little under £100.00. From software to software, prices vary. If bought, when not on a special offer, costs can double from almost £200.00; or (AUD $400) so it is wise to watch their website for a Special Offer on the software.

(Again, software is being constantly updated, so you will need to check on the internet.)

If you are going down this route to publishing, though it is not difficult to do, it does take time to learn and use. E-Commerce. Most e-book software has excellent tutorials that can take you step-by-step through the process of learning how to use their software framework.

## Marketing On The Internet

Again, this is where a hurdle can come up to selling your book. As recently as 2019, it was difficult to understand what to do next and where to go with the avenues to selling your book!

Since that time Google now have a page for authors to directly linked from Google to your website, explore this.

Other suggestions: E Bay has an on-line bookshop that has a chargeable monthly rate.

I now employ a social media marketing company to work with me in the promotion of books and the website. For me, this was easier than trying to work through the complicated maze of social media.

# Chapter Six

## Don't Forget – Plan Your Book

1. Think through your ideas before you start to write. Use Your Topics of Interest on Page 8 of this book.

2. Follow the 10 Tips on Page 9.

3. Validate Your Writing – Prove you know what you are talking about in the words you write!

4. Write clear and meaningful sentences – take your reader on a journey!

5. Relate your ideas to the story.

6. Remember to keep in mind: your marketplace.

7. Ask: can I solve their problem?

8. Start the journey of writing your book.

9. 'Timing' is important when you are writing – check your timing!

10. Look for niches in the marketplace!

11. Consider the e-book solution!

12. Are you creating a 'Must Have' book?

13. Consider – how will you stay in control of your book?

14. A few points to remember!

15. Follow the tips, modify to meet your needs, and demands.

16. Protect your Intellectual Property.

17. File your work in a logical way so that its easily accessible to you.

18. Going to the next step: Paper Back, E-commerce or Publisher?

19. Pricing your book!

20. Staying in control!

21. ISBN numbers and Legal Deposits!

22. Planning, re-reading, re-reading and planning!

Thank you for buying this book,

*Christine*

For Book Sales, Please Go To:
www.booksforreadingonline.com

**Your Notes**

www.ingramcontent.com/pod-product-compliance
Lightning Source LLC
Chambersburg PA
CBHW051540010526
44107CB00064B/2796